Little Science Stories

Push and Pull

By Amanda Gebhardt

2 Forces keep things on the move.

Can you spot each push and pull?

Look at this sled.

You can tug it up this snow hill.

Sit on it and give a kick.
It slides fast!

Look at this swing.

Tug its chains. Run and duck.

See it swing up high!

Look at this truck.

Drive it left. Back it up.

Tap it just a bit. It will go slow.

What can you do to make it race?

Word List

science words
Forces   pull
move   push

sight words
a   move
do   pull
Forces   the
give   to
go   What

Vowel Teams

/ā/ai
chains

/ī/igh
high

/o͞o/ou
you
You

/ē/ea, ee
each
keep
See

/ō/ow
slow
snow

/o͝o/oo
Look

Try It!
Push or pull an object. Then push or pull it harder. Tell what happens.

77 Words

Forces keep things on the move.

Can you spot each push and pull?

Look at this sled.

You can tug it up this snow hill.

Sit on it and give a kick. It slides fast!

Look at this swing.

Tug its chains. Run and duck.

See it swing up high!

Look at this truck.

Drive it left. Back it up.

Tap it just a bit. It will go slow.

What can you do to make it race?

Published in the United States of America by Cherry Lake Publishing Group
Ann Arbor, Michigan
www.cherrylakepublishing.com

Photo Credits: © Dvulikaia/Dreamstime.com, cover, title page; © LightField Studios/Shutterstock, 2; © vectorfusionart/Shutterstock, 3; © Olivkairishka/Shutterstock, 4; © Olivkairishka/Shutterstock, 5; © Nastyaofly/Shutterstock, 6; © A3pfamily/Shutterstock, 7; © A3pfamily/Shutterstock, 8; © A3pfamily/Shutterstock, 9; © Dvulikaia/Dreamstime.com, 10; © © Dvulikaia/Dreamstime.com, 11; © Dvulikaia/Dreamstime.com, 12; © Dvulikaia/Dreamstime.com, 13; © Sergiy Kuzmin/Shutterstock, back cover

Copyright © 2024 by Cherry Lake Publishing Group

All rights reserved. No part of this book may be reproduced or utilized in any form or by any means without written permission from the publisher.

Cherry Blossom Press is an imprint of Cherry Lake Publishing Group.

Library of Congress Cataloging-in-Publication Data

Names: Gebhardt, Amanda, author.
Title: Push and pull / written by Amanda Gebhardt.
Description: Ann Arbor, Michigan : Cherry Blossom Press, [2024] | Series: Little science stories | Audience: Grades K-1 | Summary: "Explore forces of motion in this decodable science book for beginning readers. A combination of domain-specific sight words and sequenced phonics skills builds confidence in content area reading. Bold, colorful photographs align directly with the text to help readers strengthen comprehension"– Provided by publisher.
Identifiers: LCCN 2023035050 | ISBN 9781668937679 (paperback) | ISBN 9781668940051 (ebook) | ISBN 9781668941409 (pdf)
Subjects: LCSH: Force and energy–Juvenile literature.
Classification: LCC QC73.4 .G43 2024 | DDC 531/.6–dc23/eng/20231012
LC record available at https://lccn.loc.gov/2023035050

Printed in the United States of America

Amanda Gebhardt is a curriculum writer and editor and a life-long learner. She lives in Ann Arbor, Michigan, with her husband, two kids, and one playful pup named Cookie.